COOKING
FOR TWO

Photography by Peter Barry
Designed by Richard Hawke and Claire Leighton
Edited by Jillian Stewart and Kate Cranshaw

3563
© 1994 Coombe Books
This edition published 1995 by Coombe Books for
Parragon Book Service Ltd
Unit 13-17 Avonbridge Trading Estate, Atlantic Road
Avonmouth, Bristol BS11 9QD
All rights reserved
Printed and bound in Hong Kong
ISBN 1-85813-457-9

COOKING FOR TWO

PARRAGON

Contents

Introduction

Cooking for two, whether for a mid-week supper, a light meal, or a romantic candlelit dinner, need not be a chore or a nail-biting affair – it can be great fun. For many people, particularly those who don't have much time, cooking for two has come to mean heating up a ready-made meal rather than actually preparing something. This approach, although understandable, is far from ideal. The majority of convenience meals are expensive, not always healthy, and leave a lot to be desired in terms of taste. In contrast, home-cooked meals are more economical and give far greater variety and flavour.

When cooking for two, the best dishes to choose for everyday meals, particularly if you are starting after a day's work, are those that are fairly quick and easy to prepare – the more lengthy ones can always be saved for the weekend. Rice, pasta, and salads make good accompaniments for convenient mid-week meals. If meat is on the menu for the main course, the choice of cut is, of course, crucial. The best cuts are small or individual ones, such as steaks, chops, escalopes and mince. Chicken is a particularly popular choice because it is quick and easy to cook and available in so many forms, including thighs, breasts and drumsticks. Fish is also an ideal buy, as there is little or no wastage and preparation and cooking can be very quick and simple. Game, such as quail, pheasant, pigeon and rabbit, along with duck and poussin – which take longer to prepare and cook – make ideal fare for special occasions.

To make preparation and cooking easier, it is often a good idea to make double the quantity of a recipe, or a part of it – such as the sauce – so that half can be frozen for a quick and easy meal at some later date. This allows you to maximise your time with the minimum of effort. When cooking for a special occasion, dishes that can be partly or wholly prepared in advance, such as the starter and the dessert, are obviously a great advantage, so that you don't spend all evening in the kitchen.

Cooking For Two contains recipes for all occasions and all seasons. Every recipe is set out in an easy-to-follow format and has been kitchen-tested to help give you perfect results every time. So if you need some new ideas for everyday meals, or don't know what to prepare for that special occasion dinner, look no further than *Cooking For Two*, and spice up your cooking with some exciting new dishes.

HUMMUS

A classic starter which also makes the perfect snack.

SERVES 2

120g/4oz cooked chick peas (reserve stock)
2 tbsps light tahini, (sesame paste)
Juice of 1 lemon
3 tbsps olive oil
1-2 cloves garlic, crushed
Salt to taste

1. Put the cooked chick peas into a blender together with 75ml/5 tbsps of the reserved stock.

2. Add the tahini, lemon juice, half of the olive oil, the garlic, and salt.

3. Blend until smooth, adding a little more stock if it is too thick and mint

4. Leave to stand for an hour or so to let the flavours develop.

5. Serve on individual dishes with the remaining olive oil drizzled over the top.

TIME: Preparation takes 10 minutes, standing time takes 1 hour.

SERVING IDEAS: Serve sprinkled with paprika and garnished with wedges of lemon. Accompany the hummus with warm pitta bread.

VARIATION: Use canned chick peas for a quick version and use some of the liquid from the can instead of stock.

STUFFED COURGETTES

*Serve as a starter, or accompany with a parsley sauce
and potatoes for a light lunch.*

SERVES 2

---

2 medium courgettes
1 tbsp olive oil
½ onion, very finely chopped
60g/2oz carrots, grated
¼ tsp paprika
½ tsp cumin seeds
Pinch turmeric
60g/2oz creamed coconut, grated

---

1. Wash the courgettes and cut in half lengthwise.

2. Using a teaspoon, remove the flesh leaving about 5mm/¼-inch shell.

3. Chop the flesh finely.

4. Heat the oil in a frying pan and sauté the onion for a few minutes.

5. Add the carrots, courgette flesh and spices and cook, stirring frequently, for a further 5 minutes or until softened.

6. Remove from the heat and stir in the creamed coconut.

7. Divide the mixture between the courgette shells making sure that it covers the exposed part of the flesh.

8. Place the courgettes in a greased ovenproof casserole and cook at 190°C/375°F/Gas Mark 5 for 45 minutes until the courgette shells are soft.

9. Serve immediately.

TIME: Preparation takes 10 minutes, cooking takes 55 minutes.

COOK'S TIP: Creamed coconut can be bought at delicatessens, health food shops and most major supermarkets.

11

FRESH CREAMED MUSHROOMS

A versatile recipe that's good as a starter, a side dish or a sauce.

SERVES 2

225g/8oz even-sized button mushrooms
2 tsps lemon juice
15g/½oz butter or margarine
2 tsps flour
Freshly grated nutmeg
Salt and white pepper
1 small bay leaf
1 blade mace
140ml/¼ pint double cream
2 tsps dry sherry (optional)

1. Wash the mushrooms quickly and dry them well. Trim the stems level with the caps. Leave the mushrooms whole if small, and halve or quarter if large. Toss with the lemon juice and set aside. The mushroom stalks can be chopped and added to soups or sauces.

2. In a medium saucepan, melt the butter or margarine and stir in the flour. Cook, stirring gently, for about 1 minute. Remove from the heat, add some nutmeg, salt and pepper, the bay leaf and mace and gradually stir in the cream.

3. Return the pan to the heat and bring to the boil, stirring constantly. Allow to boil for about 1 minute, or until thickened. Reduce the heat and add the mushrooms. Simmer gently, covered for about 5 minutes, or until the mushrooms are tender.

4. Add the sherry, if using, during the last few minutes of cooking. Remove the bay leaf and blade mace. Sprinkle with additional grated nutmeg before serving.

TIME: Preparation takes about 20 minutes and cooking takes about 7 minutes.

COOK'S TIP: If the mushrooms are clean, just wipe over with damp cloth. If washing is necessary, rinse them very quickly and pat dry quickly, as mushrooms absorb water easily.

VARIATION: The recipe may be used as a sauce for chicken or ham.

SERVING IDEAS: Serve on hot toast or in individual ramekin dishes or scallop shells, accompanied with hot buttered toast or melba toast.

ARTICHAUTS AIOLI

Home-made mayonnaise is in a class by itself. With the addition of garlic, it makes a perfect sauce for artichokes – a typically Provençal starter.

SERVES 2

2 medium-sized globe artichokes
1 slice lemon
1 bay leaf
Pinch salt

Sauce Aioli

1 egg yolk
1 clove garlic, crushed
Salt and pepper
140ml/¼ pint olive oil
Lemon juice, to taste
Chervil leaves, to garnish

1. To prepare the artichokes, break off the stems and twist to remove any tough fibres. Trim the base so that the artichokes will stand upright. Trim the points from all the leaves and wash the artichokes well.

2. Bring a large saucepan or stock pot full of water to the boil with the slice of lemon, the bay leaf and a pinch of salt.

3. When the water is boiling, add the artichokes. Allow to cook for 25 minutes over a moderate heat. While the artichokes are cooking, prepare the sauce.

4. Whisk the egg yolk and garlic with a pinch of salt and pepper in a deep bowl, or in a liquidiser or food processor.

5. Add the olive oil a few drops at a time while whisking by hand, or in a thin, steady stream with the machine running. If preparing the sauce by hand, once half the oil is added, the remainder may be added in a thin steady stream.

6. Add lemon juice once the sauce becomes very thick. When all the oil has been added, adjust the seasoning and add more lemon juice to taste.

7. When the artichokes are cooked, the bottom leaves will pull away easily. Remove them from the water with a draining spoon and drain upside-down on kitchen paper or in a colander. Allow to cool and serve with the sauce aioli. Garnish with chervil.

TIME: Preparation will take about 30 minutes and cooking about 25 minutes.

COOK'S TIP: If this sauce or other mayonnaise needs to be thinned for coating, mix with a little hot water. A damp cloth under the mixing bowl will stop it spinning when making mayonnaise by hand.

WATCHPOINT: The sauce will curdle if the oil is added too quickly. If it does, whisk another egg yolk and gradually beat the curdled mixture into it; the sauce should come together again.

IMPERIAL ASPARAGUS

Fresh asparagus is delicious. Serve as an impressive starter to a special meal.

SERVES 2

460g/1lb green asparagus
25g/¾oz butter or margarine
1½ tbsps flour
140ml/¼ pint chicken stock
75ml/5 tbsps white wine
1 egg yolk
2 tbsps double cream
Salt and white pepper
Pinch salt

---

1. Break off the bottom woody part of the asparagus stems then trim the ends to make the spears the same length. Using a swivel vegetable peeler, pare the stalks up to the tips.

2. To cook the asparagus, tie the spears in a bundle and stand them upright in a deep saucepan of lightly salted, boiling water. Alternatively, place the spears in a large frying pan of boiling, salted water, half on and half off the heat, with the tips of the asparagus off the heat.

3. Cook, uncovered, for about 12 minutes, or until the asparagus is tender. Drain and reserve the cooking liquid. Keep the asparagus warm in a covered serving dish.

4. Meanwhile, prepare the sauce. Melt the butter in a heavy-based saucepan and stir in the flour off the heat. Gradually beat in the chicken stock and add the wine. Stir until the sauce is smooth.

5. Bring the sauce to the boil, stirring constantly, and allow to boil for about 1-2 minutes, or until thickened.

6. Beat the egg yolk and cream together and add a few spoonfuls of the hot sauce. Return the egg and cream mixture to the pan, stirring constantly. Reheat if necessary, but do not allow the sauce to boil once the egg is added. Add salt and white pepper and a pinch of sugar if needed. Pour over the asparagus to serve.

TIME: Preparation takes about 30 minutes, cooking takes about 12-15 minutes for the asparagus and about 10 minutes for the sauce.

VARIATION: Use white asparagus instead of green.

SERVING IDEAS: This dish could also be served as a side dish with ham and new potatoes.

FRIED AUBERGINE WITH TZATZIKI

The fresh taste of cucumber, mint and yogurt is the perfect complement to rich, fried aubergine slices.

SERVES 2

---

2 small or 1 medium sized aubergine
Salt and pepper
30g/1oz plain flour
Vegetable oil for frying

Tzatziki
¼ cucumber, finely chopped or grated
Salt and pepper
1 tbsp olive oil
1 tsp wine vinegar
1 clove garlic, crushed
140ml/¼ pint natural yogurt
10ml/2 tsps chopped, fresh mint
Whole mint leaves, for garnishing

---

1. Wash the aubergines and dry them. Cut into 5mm/¼-inch rounds and lightly score the surfaces with a sharp knife. Sprinkle both sides with salt and leave to drain in a colander for 30 minutes.

2. Sprinkle the cucumber lightly with salt and leave in a colander, slightly weighted down, to drain for 30 minutes.

3. Meanwhile, mix the oil and vinegar until well blended, add the crushed garlic and mix in the yogurt and mint.

4. Rinse both the aubergine slices and cucumber to remove the salt, pat the aubergine slices dry on kitchen paper and squeeze excess moisture from the cucumber. Add the cucumber to the tzatziki.

5. Mix the salt and pepper together with the flour and coat the aubergine slices well. Heat the oil to 180°C/350°F and fry the aubergine a few slices at a time. Remove them with a draining spoon to kitchen paper and sprinkle lightly with salt. Continue with the remaining slices.

6. To serve, arrange the aubergine slices on individual plates or one large plate and add the tzatziki. Garnish with mint leaves.

TIME: Preparation takes about 30 minutes, cooking takes about 2-3 minutes per batch of aubergine slices.

COOK'S TIP: Sprinkling aubergine and cucumber with salt before using draws out excess moisture and bitter juices. Sprinkling deep-fried food lightly with salt while it stands helps to draw out excess fat.

VARIATION: Courgettes may be used instead of aubergines. Top and tail the courgettes and slice them into 3 or 4 lengthwise slices. Courgettes do not have to be sprinkled with salt and left to stand.

FRESH TOMATO OMELETTE

*Omelettes can make substantial lunches or light meals and can be varied by
using different fillings.*

SERVES 2

460g/1lb fresh tomatoes
4 eggs
60ml/4 tbsps water
½ tsp fresh chopped basil
Salt and freshly ground black pepper
2 tbsps olive or vegetable oil
½ tsp fresh chopped basil to garnish

1. Cut a small cross into the skin of each tomato and plunge them into boiling water. Leave for 30 seconds, then remove them with a draining spoon to cold water.

2. Using a sharp knife carefully peel away the tomato skins and discard them.

3. Cut the tomatoes in half and remove and discard the seeds, juice and any tough core. Cut the flesh into thin strips.

4. Break the eggs into a bowl and whisk in the water and chopped basil. Season with salt and pepper and continue whisking until the egg mixture is frothy.

5. Heat the oil in a large frying pan, then pour in the egg mixture.

6. Using a palette knife, stir the egg mixture around the frying pan for about 2-3 minutes, or until the eggs are beginning to set.

7. Spread the tomato strips over the partially cooked eggs, and continue cooking without stirring until the eggs have completely set and the tomatoes are just warmed through.

8. Sprinkle with the additional chopped basil just before serving.

TIME: Preparation takes about 25 minutes, cooking takes about 5 minutes.

VARIATION: Add 1 clove of crushed garlic to the egg mixture and sprinkle with 1 tbsp grated Parmesan before serving.

SERVING IDEA: Cut the omelette into wedges and serve straight from the frying pan.

PRAWN PROVENÇALE

Deceptively simple, this dish combines ingredients that are easy to find and that almost everyone enjoys.

SERVES 2

---

2 tbsps oil
1 large green pepper, cut into 2.5cm/1 inch
  pieces
1 stick celery, sliced
1 medium onion, diced
1 clove garlic, crushed
1 × 400g/14oz can tomatoes
1 bay leaf
Pinch cayenne pepper, or dash of Tabasco
  sauce
Pinch salt and pepper
Pinch thyme
1 tbsp cornflour mixed with 1½ tbsps dry
  white wine
225g/8oz cooked, peeled prawns
Cooked rice, to serve

---

1. Place the oil in a large saucepan and add the vegetables. Cook for a few minutes over gentle heat and add the garlic.

2. Add the tomatoes and their juice, breaking up the tomatoes with a fork or a potato masher. Add the bay leaf, cayenne pepper or Tabasco, seasoning and thyme, and bring to the boil. Allow to simmer for about 5 minutes, uncovered.

3. Mix a few spoonfuls of the hot tomato liquid with the cornflour mixture and then return it to the saucepan. Bring to the boil, stirring constantly until thickened.

4. Simmer over a gentle heat for about 15 minutes. Add the prawns and heat through gently for 5 minutes.

5. Remove the bay leaf before serving, and spoon the sauce over rice.

TIME: Preparation takes about 25 minutes and cooking takes about 20-30 minutes. Rice will take about 15-20 minutes to cook.

COOK'S TIP: Do not allow prawns or other shellfish to cook too rapidly or for too long, as this will toughen them.

VARIATION: An equal amount of cooked white fish, or even boned and cooked chicken, can be substituted for the prawns.

SALMON PIES

This recipe uses economical canned pink salmon in a very unusual and tasty way.

SERVES 2

Pastry

120g/4oz plain flour, sifted
Pinch salt
60g-90g/2-3oz butter or margarine
Cold water

Filling

1 medium can pink salmon
1½ tbsps oil
1½ tbsps flour
½ small green pepper, finely diced
1 spring onion, finely chopped
1 stick celery, finely chopped
140ml/¼ pint milk
Salt and pepper

1. Sift the flour in a bowl with a pinch of salt and rub in the butter or margarine until the mixture resembles breadcrumbs. Add enough cold water to bring the mixture together. Knead into a ball, wrap well and chill for about 30 minutes before use.

2. Drain the salmon and remove any skin and bones.

3. Heat the oil for the filling in a small saucepan and stir in the flour. Cook slowly, stirring constantly until the flour turns a rich dark brown.

4. Add the remaining filling ingredients, stirring constantly while adding the milk. Bring to the boil, reduce the heat and cook for about 5 minutes. Add the salmon to the sauce.

5. Divide the pastry into two and roll out each portion on a lightly-floured surface to about 5mm/¼-inch thick.

6. Line 2 individual flan tins or pie dishes with the pastry, pushing it carefully into the base and up the sides, taking care not to stretch it. Trim off the excess pastry and reserve.

7. Place a sheet of greaseproof paper or foil on the pastry cases and pour on rice, pasta or baking beans to come halfway up the sides. Bake the pastry blind for about 10 minutes in a preheated oven at 200°C/400°F/Gas Mark 6.

8. Remove the paper and beans and bake the cases for an additional 5 minutes to cook the base.

9. Spoon in the filling and roll out any trimmings to make lattice patterns on top. Bake for a further 10 minutes to brown the lattice and heat the filling. Cool slightly before serving.

TIME: Preparation takes about 30 minutes and cooking takes about 10 minutes for the filling and 25 minutes to finish the dish.

COOK'S TIP: Baking the pastry blind helps it to crisp on the base and brown evenly without overcooking the filling.

SERVING IDEAS: Serve as a light main course with a salad or with new potatoes and broccoli.

MEDITERRANEAN AUBERGINES

*These delicious stuffed aubergines make a delicious and unusual
lunch dish for two.*

SERVES 2

2 small aubergines
30g/1oz butter or margarine
1 small onion, finely chopped
1 clove garlic, crushed
120g/4oz tomatoes
150g/5oz long grain rice, cooked
2 tsps fresh chopped marjoram
Pinch cinnamon
Salt and freshly ground black pepper

1. Wrap the aubergines in aluminium foil and bake in an oven preheated to 180°C/350°F/Gas Mark 4, for 20 minutes to soften. Allow to cool.

2. Cut the aubergines in half, then using a serrated teaspoon or grapefruit knife, carefully scoop out the pulp leaving a 1.25cm/½-inch border of flesh to form a shell.

3. Melt the butter in a frying pan and gently sauté the onion and garlic until they are just soft.

4. Chop the aubergine pulp roughly and stir into the pan. Cover and cook for about 5 minutes.

5. Cut a small cross in the skins of the tomatoes and plunge them into boiling water for 30 seconds.

6. Remove the tomatoes from the water and carefully peel away the skin using a sharp knife.

7. Quarter the tomatoes and remove and discard the pips. Chop the tomato flesh roughly and stir into the cooked aubergine and onion mixture, along with the rice, marjoram and cinnamon. Season with salt and pepper.

8. Carefully pile the rice filling back into the aubergine shells and arrange them on an ovenproof dish or baking tray. Cover with aluminium foil.

9. Return to the oven and bake a further 20 minutes. Serve hot, garnished with a little finely chopped parsley if wished.

TIME: Preparation takes 25 minutes, cooking takes about 40 minutes.

PREPARATION: Take care not to split the aubergine shells when scooping out the pulp.

VARIATION: 60g/2oz mature Cheddar cheese can be added to the filling.

KEDGEREE

*This traditional breakfast dish, which dates back to the time of the Indian Raj,
makes an excellent lunch or supper dish.*

SERVES 2

90g/3oz rice
30g/1oz butter
½ small onion, sliced
60g/2oz mushrooms
15g/½oz flour
¼ tsp curry powder
280ml/½ pint milk
175g/6oz smoked haddock
1 tbsp lemon juice
60g/2oz peeled prawns
Salt and pepper
75ml/5 tbsps single cream, optional
2 hard-boiled eggs, sliced or quartered
1 tbsp parsley, chopped

---

1. Cook the rice for about 12 minutes, or until tender. Drain under hot water to remove the excess starch and leave to dry.

2. Melt the butter in a large pan, add the onion and sauté until golden brown.

3. Add mushrooms and cook for a few seconds before stirring in the flour. Add the curry powder and cook for a minute or two.

4. Gradually work in the cold milk until all is incorporated. Bring to the boil, then simmer for 5 minutes, stirring constantly, until thickened.

5. Skin the smoked haddock, cut into small pieces, add to the sauce and continue to cook.

6. Once the fish is cooked, add the lemon juice, prawns and salt and pepper to taste. Stir in the cooked rice, and if the sauce seems too thick, add the single cream.

7. Mound the kedgeree into a heated serving dish. Sprinkle on the chopped parsley and garnish with the hard-boiled eggs.

TIME: Preparation takes about 15 minutes and cooking takes 20 minutes.

VARIATION: Although not authentic, canned tuna makes a quick and convenient substitute for the haddock and prawns.

SERVING IDEAS: Serve with a green salad and crusty bread.

AUBERGINE AND CHICKEN CHILLI

This unusual dish is both delicious and filling. Serve on its own with boiled rice, or part of a more extensive chinese-style meal.

SERVES 2

---

1 medium aubergine
2 tbsps sesame oil
1 clove garlic, crushed
2 spring onions, diagonally sliced
½ green chilli, finely chopped
175g/6oz boned and skinned chicken
    breast, thinly sliced
60ml/4 tbsps light soy sauce
30ml/2 tbsps stock, or water
1 tbsp tomato purée
1 tsp cornflour
Sugar to taste

---

1. Cut the aubergine into quarters lengthways, using a sharp knife. Slice the aubergine quarters into chunks about 1.25cm/½-inch thick.

2. Put the aubergine into a bowl and sprinkle liberally with salt. Stir well to coat evenly. Cover with cling film and leave to stand for 30 minutes.

3. Rinse the aubergine very thoroughly under running water, then pat dry with a clean tea-cloth.

4. Heat half of the oil in a wok, or large frying pan, and gently cook the garlic until it is soft, but not coloured.

5. Add the aubergine chunks to the wok and cook, stirring frequently, for 3-4 minutes.

6. Stir the spring onions and the chilli into the cooked aubergine, and cook for a further 1 minute. Remove the aubergine and onion from the pan and set aside, keeping warm.

7. Heat the remaining oil in the wok, and fry the chicken pieces for approximately 2 minutes or until they have turned white and are cooked thoroughly.

8. Return the aubergine and onions to the pan and cook, stirring continuously, for 2 minutes or until heated through completely.

9. Mix together the remaining ingredients and pour these over the chicken and aubergine in the wok, stirring constantly until the sauce has thickened and cleared. Serve immediately.

TIME: Preparation takes about 10 minutes, plus 30 minutes standing time. Cooking takes about 10 minutes.

COOK'S TIP: The vegetables can be prepared well in advance, but the aubergines should be removed from the salt after 30 minutes, or they will become too dehydrated.

VARIATION: Use turkey instead of chicken in this recipe, and courgettes in place of the aubergines.

LIVER AND BACON KEBABS

These economical and delicious kebabs are exceptionally nutritious and are also very quick and easy to prepare.

SERVES 2

275g/10oz lambs' liver, trimmed
120g/4oz lean back bacon
60g/2oz small button mushrooms, trimmed
2 tbsps olive oil
60g/2oz very fine wholemeal breadcrumbs
½ tsp paprika pepper
Freshly ground sea salt

1. Wipe the liver and cut away any coarse tubes.

2. Cut the liver into 2.5cm/1-inch cubes.

3. De-rind the bacon and cut each rasher in half lengthways. Roll each bacon strip into small bacon rolls.

4. Thread the bacon rolls, liver and mushrooms alternately onto 4 skewers. Brush the meat and vegetables with a little of the oil.

5. On a plate, mix together the breadcrumbs, paprika and salt. Turn the kebabs in the breadcrumbs until they are evenly coated.

6. Arrange the kebabs on the lightly oiled grill pan and cook for 5-10 minutes under a medium preheated grill, turning the kebabs frequently, and brushing them with any of the oil that remains, to prevent them burning.

TIME: Preparation will take about 20 minutes, and cooking takes about 5-10 minutes.

VARIATION: Use courgettes or peppers instead of the mushrooms, if liked.

SERVING IDEAS: Serve the kebabs on a bed of rice, mixed with the vegetables of your choice.

PRAWN RISOTTO

High in fibre and in flavour, prawn risotto is both delicious and healthy.

SERVES 2

225g/8oz unpeeled prawns
½ glass white wine
2 fresh tomatoes
2 cloves garlic
1 small onion
2 tbsps olive oil
1 tbsp chopped fresh parsley
90g/3oz brown rice
1 tsp tomato purée
Freshly ground sea salt and black pepper
1 tbsp grated Parmesan cheese

1. Peel the prawns, leaving 4 unpeeled for a garnish. Put the prawn shells and the wine into a saucepan and bring to the boil. Remove the pan from the heat and allow to cool completely before straining, and reserving the liquid.

2. Chop the tomatoes roughly, and remove the woody cores. Chop the garlic and onion.

3. Heat the olive oil in a large frying pan, or saucepan. Cook the onion and garlic gently in the oil, without browning them. Stir in the parsley and cook for about 30 seconds.

4. Add the rice to the fried onion, and stir well to coat the grains with the oil.

5. Add the reserved liquid, tomato purée, tomatoes and just enough cold water to cover the rice.

6. Season the rice with salt and pepper, and cook for about 30 minutes, until all the water is absorbed and the rice is tender.

7. When the rice is cooked, stir in the peeled prawns and the cheese, and heat through gently. Pile into a serving dish, and top with the unpeeled prawns as a garnish.

TIME: Preparation takes about 15 minutes, and cooking takes about 35 minutes.

SERVING IDEAS: Serve the risotto with a fresh mixed salad.

PREPARATION: If all the water is absorbed before the rice is cooked, add a little more, but take care not to add too much, or the rice will become stodgy.

CHICKEN WITH WALNUTS AND CELERY

Oyster sauce lends a subtle, slightly salty taste to this Cantonese dish.

SERVES 2

225g/8oz boned chicken, cut into 2.5cm/1-inch pieces

2 tsps soy sauce

2 tsps brandy

1 tsp cornflour

Salt and pepper

1 tbsp oil

1 clove garlic

60g/2oz walnut halves

3 sticks celery, cut in diagonal slices

2 tsps oyster sauce

120ml/4 fl oz water or chicken stock

1. Combine the chicken with the soy sauce, brandy, cornflour, salt and pepper.

2. Heat a wok and add the oil and garlic. Cook for about 1 minute to flavour the oil.

3. Remove the garlic and add the chicken in two batches. Stir-fry quickly without allowing the chicken to brown.

4. Remove the chicken and add the walnuts to the wok. Cook for about 2 minutes until the walnuts are slightly brown and crisp.

5. Add the celery to the wok and cook for about 1 minute. Add the oyster sauce and water and bring to the boil. Return the chicken to the pan and stir to coat all the ingredients well. Serve immediately.

TIME: Preparation takes about 20 minutes, cooking takes about 8 minutes.

WATCHPOINT: Nuts can burn very easily. Stir them constantly for even browning.

VARIATION: Almonds or cashew nuts may be used instead of the walnuts. If the cashew nuts are already roasted, add them along with the celery.

SERVING IDEAS: Serve with boiled or fried rice.

BUYING GUIDE: Oyster sauce, made from oysters and soy sauce, is available from major supermarkets.

BACON, PEPPER AND TOMATO OMELETTE

Omelettes make a quick and nutritious meal. Serve with a salad and crusty bread.

SERVES 2

4 rashers back bacon, diced
½ small onion, chopped
½ small green pepper, chopped
1 tomato, seeded and diced
3 eggs, beaten
Salt and pepper
1 tbsp grated cheese
Parsley, to garnish

1. Heat a medium-sized frying pan or omelette pan, add the bacon and sauté slowly until the fat is rendered.

2. Turn up the heat and cook until the bacon begins to brown and crisp. Add the onion and green pepper and cook to soften and finish off the bacon.

3. Mix the tomato with the eggs, salt, and pepper, and cheese. Pour into the pan and stir once or twice with a fork to mix all the ingredients. Cook until lightly browned on the underside.

4. Place under a pre-heated grill and cook the top quickly until brown and slightly puffy.

5. Garnish with parsley, cut into wedges and serve immediately.

TIME: Preparation takes about 25 minutes and cooking takes about 10-15 minutes.

COOK'S TIP: 1 tbsp of water added to the eggs before beating will produce a lighter, fluffier omelette.

ONION, EGG AND TOMATO BAKE

This dish makes a great lunch or supper dish that is quick and easy to prepare.

SERVES 2

2 tbsps olive oil
2 medium onions, sliced
30g/1oz wholemeal flour
140ml/¼ pint milk
Freshly milled sea salt and black pepper, to
taste
4 eggs, hard-boiled
2 tomatoes, thinly sliced
3 tbsps fresh wholemeal breadcrumbs
1 tbsp freshly grated Parmesan cheese

1. Heat the oil in a pan and sauté the onions gently until they are softened, but not coloured. Remove from the pan with a slotted spoon and set aside.

2. Stir the flour into the oil in the pan, and cook for 1 minute. Add the milk gradually, beating well between additions. Simmer gently for 2-3 minutes, stirring continuously.

3. Add the onions to the sauce and season well to taste.

4. Cut the eggs in half and remove the yolks. Push the yolks through a sieve and set aside.

5. Rinse and chop the egg whites and place them in the bottom of a medium-sized ovenproof dish.

6. Cover the chopped egg whites with the onion mixture and then top this with a layer of sliced tomatoes.

7. Put the breadcrumbs and Parmesan cheese into a mixing bowl, and stir in the sieved egg yolks, mixing well, until all the ingredients are thoroughly incorporated. Sprinkle this over the layer of tomatoes.

8. Bake in a preheated oven at 200°C/400°F/Gas Mark 6, for 15-20 minutes, or until golden brown.

TIME: Preparation takes about 15 minutes, and cooking takes 20-25 minutes.

PREPARATION: If there is not enough oil left in the frying pan after the onions have been removed, heat a further 1 tbsp of olive oil before adding the flour.

SERVING IDEA: Serve with a crisp green salad.

GARNISHED PEPPER STEAK

This is an unusual German recipe not only because of its garnish, but also because beef is so seldom used.

SERVES 2

1 clove garlic, crushed
Salt and freshly ground black pepper
2 sirloin or rump steaks about 120g/4oz
    each in weight
Oil

Sauce
1 shallot, finely chopped
2 tbsps capers
60g/2oz mushrooms, sliced
1 tbsp flour
140ml/¼ pint beef stock
2 tsps German mustard
1 tsp Worcestershire sauce
60ml/4 tbsps German white wine
1 tsp lemon juice
Pinch each of thyme and rosemary

Garnish
4 baby corn cobs, halved
½ green pepper and ½ red pepper, thinly
    sliced
2 peperonata, stem and seeds removed and
    cut in half
2 ripe tomatoes, skinned, seeded and cut
    into thin strips
60g/2oz bone marrow (optional)

1. Rub the crushed garlic, salt and pepper into both sides of each steak. Heat a large frying pan and brush the surface lightly with oil.

2. Place the steaks in the hot pan and press them down firmly with a fish slice to seal. Turn over and repeat. Remove the steaks to a plate and add 1 tbsp of oil to the pan.

3. Add the shallot, capers and mushrooms and cook for about 1 minute. Sprinkle on the flour and cook to brown slightly.

4. Pour on the stock, stirring in well, add the remaining sauce ingredients and bring to the boil.

5. Add the corn and peppers to the sauce and return the steaks to the pan. Cook for 6-8 minutes, or until until the steaks are cooked to your liking. Add the remaining ingredients to the sauce, slicing the bone marrow, if using.

6. Transfer the steaks to a heated serving plate, reheat the sauce and spoon over the steaks to serve.

TIME: Preparation takes about 30 minutes, cooking takes about 20 minutes in total.

PREPARATION: Sealing the steaks on both sides helps to seal in the meat juices.

LIME-ROASTED CHICKEN

This simply made, but unusual, main course is very low in calories and high in tangy flavour.

SERVES 2

2 chicken breast portions, each weighing
    about 225g/8oz
Salt and freshly ground black pepper
2 limes
1 tsp white wine vinegar
3 tbsps olive oil
1 tsp fresh chopped basil

1. Rub the chicken portions all over with salt and black pepper. Place in a shallow ovenproof dish, and set aside.

2. Pare the rind from 1 of the limes into thin strips, using a lemon zester, then cut the lime in half and squeeze the juice.

3. Add the lime juice to the vinegar and 1½ tbsps of the olive oil in a small dish, along with the strips of rind, and mix well.

4. Pour the oil and lime juice mixture over the chicken portions in the dish. Cover and refrigerate for about 4 hours or overnight.

5. Uncover the dish and baste the chicken well with the marinade mixture. Cook in a preheated oven at 190°C/375°F/Gas Mark 5, for 30-35 minutes, or until the chicken is well roasted and tender.

6. In the meantime, cut off all the rind and white pith from the remaining lime. Cut the lime crosswise into thin slices using a sharp knife.

7. Heat the remaining oil in a small frying pan and add the lime slices and basil. Cook quickly for 1 minute, or until the basil becomes aromatic and the lime just begins to soften.

8. Serve the chicken portions on a platter, garnished with the fried lime slices and a little extra fresh basil, if wished.

TIME: Preparation takes 25 minutes, plus 4 hours marinating time. Cooking takes 40 minutes.

PREPARATION: Allow the chicken to come to room temperature before cooking.

WATCHPOINT: To see if the chicken is cooked, test it with a skewer at its thickest point. If the juices run clear, it is ready.

VARIATION: Use lemons instead of limes, and thyme instead of basil.

STUFFED, BAKED TROUT

*Three kinds of ground pepper make this stuffing quite hot. Cut down the amount
a bit, if you prefer a mild flavour.*

SERVES 2

2 whole trout, about 225g/8oz each
60g/2oz butter or margarine
1 small onion, finely chopped
1 stick celery, finely chopped
½ small red pepper, finely chopped
2 spring onions, finely chopped
1 clove garlic, crushed
⅛ tsp white pepper
⅛ tsp cayenne pepper
⅛ tsp black pepper
1 tsp chopped fresh dill
2 tsps chopped parsley
60g/2oz dry breadcrumbs
1 small egg, lightly beaten
Pinch salt

1. Wash the trout well inside and pat dry.

2. Melt half the butter or margarine in a medium saucepan. Add the onion, celery, red pepper, spring onions and garlic. Cook over a moderate heat for about 3 minutes to soften the vegetables. Stir in the white pepper, cayenne pepper and black pepper, dill and parsley.

3. Remove from the heat, add the breadcrumbs and gradually beat in the egg, adding just enough to hold the stuffing ingredients together. Season with salt.

4. Fill the cavity of each trout with an equal amount of the stuffing and place in a baking dish.

5. Dot over the remaining butter and bake, uncovered, in a preheated oven at 180°C/350°F/Gas Mark 4 for about 25 minutes. Brown under a preheated grill before serving, if wished.

TIME: Preparation takes about 30 minutes and cooking takes about 30 minutes.

VARIATION: Other varieties of fish, such as sea bass or grey mullet can also be used.

SERVING IDEAS: Serve with sautéed or boiled new potatoes, and mange tout peas.

ZIGEUNERSCHNITZEL

In this traditional German veal escalope dish a Hungarian influence is evident with the use of paprika and peppers.

SERVES 2

4 small or 2 large veal escalopes
Seasoned flour
25g/¾oz butter or margarine
½ onion
½ red and ½ green pepper, thinly sliced
1 tbsp flour
2 tsps paprika
75-140ml/3-5 fl oz beef stock
75ml/5 tbsps natural yogurt

1. Bat the escalopes out if wished. Dredge in seasoned flour and shake off the excess.

2. Melt the butter or margarine in a large frying pan and, when foaming, place in the escalopes. Lower the heat and brown on both sides. Remove and keep warm.

3. Slice the onion thinly and add to the pan. Add the pepper slices and sauté for about 3 minutes. Remove and set aside with the veal.

4. Add the flour to the pan and allow it to cook slowly until golden brown. Add the paprika and cook for 1 minute.

5. Whisk in the stock gradually to prevent lumps forming, and bring to the boil. Replace the veal and vegetables, cover and cook for 6-8 minutes, or until the veal is tender.

6. Beat the yogurt until smooth and drizzle over the veal to serve.

TIME: Preparation takes about 15 minutes, cooking takes about 15 minutes. Veal dries out very quickly, so brown slowly to avoid toughening.

PREPARATION: Always remove the white pith from inside the peppers as this tends to be bitter. This dish may be prepared in advance and reheated slowly before serving. Do not add the yogurt until ready to serve.

COOK'S TIP: If the yogurt is too thick to drizzle properly, thin with a little water or milk. Cook paprika and most spices briefly before adding any liquid to the recipe. This will develop the flavour and eliminate any harsh taste.

PEPPERED STEAK

A classic way of serving steak, peppered steaks are simple to prepare and wonderful to eat.

SERVES 2

2 rump, or fillet steaks
Oil, for frying
1 tbsp black peppercorns, lightly crushed
60g/2oz butter
Salt
2 tbsps brandy
2 tbsps single cream
Watercress, to garnish

1. Brush the steaks on both sides with some oil, then coat with the black peppercorns. Crush these into the steak with a steak hammer.

2. Over a high heat, melt the butter in a frying pan and cook the steaks for about 1½ minutes on each side.

3. Reduce the heat and cook for a further 2 minutes for a rare steak, 3 minutes for a medium steak, or 7 minutes for a well-done steak. Season with salt.

4. Warm the brandy in a small pan. Taking great care, set the brandy alight and pour it over the steaks.

5. When the flames die down, remove the steaks to a warmed serving dish. Keep warm.

6. Stir the cream into the juices in the frying pan and heat gently for a few minutes.

7. Pour the sauce over the steak

TIME: Preparation takes about 15 minutes, and cooking takes between 5 and 15 minutes, depending on whether a rare, medium or well-done steak is required.

PREPARATION: If you prefer, the steaks can be grilled, instead of fried. The cooking times should be about the same, and the sauce can be prepared separately.

VARIATION: If you can get them, use fresh green peppercorns in place of the black ones.

SERVING IDEAS: Serve with new potatoes, or French fries and a large, fresh salad.

GINGERNUT PORK CHOPS

Ginger-flavoured biscuits give a spicy lift to pork chop gravy, thickening it at the same time.

SERVES 2

2 even-sized pork chops, loin or shoulder
½ tsp ground black pepper
Pinch salt
½ tsp ground ginger
¼ tsp each ground coriander, paprika, and
　　dried sage
Pinch dried thyme
1 tbsp oil
15g/½ oz butter
½ small onion, finely chopped
1 stick celery, finely chopped
1 clove garlic, crushed
200ml/7 fl oz chicken stock
6 gingernut biscuits

1. Trim the chops of any excess fat. Mix together the seasoning, herbs and spices and press the mixture firmly onto both sides of the chops.

2. Heat the oil in a frying pan and, when hot, add the chops. Brown on both sides and remove to a plate.

3. Add the butter to the frying pan and, when foaming, add the onion, celery and garlic. Cook to soften, then pour on the stock.

4. Return the chops to the pan, cover and cook for about 30-40 minutes, or until tender.

5. When the chops are cooked, remove them to a serving dish and keep warm. Place the gingernut biscuits in a plastic bag and use a rolling pin to crush them. Stir the crushed biscuits into the pan juices and bring to the boil.

6. Stir constantly to allow the biscuits to soften and thicken the liquid. Boil rapidly for about 3 minutes to reduce, then pour over the chops to serve.

TIME: Preparation takes about 20 minutes and cooking takes about 50 minutes.

VARIATION: Chicken or rabbit may be used in place of the pork.

COOK'S TIP: The gingernuts should thicken the cooking liquid sufficiently. If not, combine 1 tsp cornflour with 2 tsps water and some of the hot cooking liquid. Return to the pan and bring to the boil, stirring constantly until thickened and cleared.

TOMATO FISH STEW

Cook any white fish you like in this tomato sauce. Serve with rice or potatoes.

SERVES 2

1 whole plaice, filleted, skin and bones reserved
1 bay leaf, 1 sprig thyme and 2 parsley stalks
1 slice onion
1 lemon slice
3 black peppercorns
200ml/7 fl oz water
3 tbsps oil
3 tbsps flour
½ large green pepper, finely chopped
1 small onion, finely chopped
1 stick celery, finely chopped
460g/1lb canned tomatoes
1 tbsp tomato purée
Pinch salt and allspice
3 tbsps white wine
1 tbsp chopped parsley

1. Place the fish trimmings, herbs, onion, lemon slice, peppercorns and water into a saucepan. Bring to the boil, then simmer for 20 minutes. Strain and reserve.

2. Heat the oil and add the flour. Cook slowly, stirring constantly, until golden brown.

3. Add the green pepper, onion and celery, and cook until the flour is a rich dark brown and the vegetables have softened.

4. Add the reserved stock and the canned tomatoes, tomato purée, salt and allspice. Bring to the boil and then simmer until thick. Add the wine.

5. Cut the fish fillets into 5cm/2-inch pieces and add to the tomato mixture. Cook slowly for about 20 minutes, or until the fish is tender. Gently stir in the parsley, taking care that the fish does not break up. Adjust the seasoning and serve.

TIME: Preparation takes about 30 minutes and cooking takes about 20 minutes for the fish stock and 20 minutes to finish the dish.

PREPARATION: The fish stock can be prepared a day in advance and refrigerated. It can also be frozen.

VARIATION: The wine may be replaced with 1 tbsp lemon juice and 2 tbsps water.

PEPPERED FILLET OF LAMB WITH FRUIT

In Catalonia, on the border of France, meat cooked with fruit is extremely popular.

SERVES 2

120g/4oz dried fruit salad
2 tsps coarsely crushed black peppercorns
460g/1lb lamb neck fillets
30g/1oz butter or margarine
1 tbsp flour
140ml/¼ pint light stock
75ml/5 tbsps medium dry sherry
Pinch salt
2 tbsps double cream
Coriander leaves to garnish

---

1. Place the fruit salad in a saucepan, cover with water and bring to the boil. Once the water boils, remove from the heat and leave to soak for about 2 hours.

2. Sprinkle the black peppercorns onto the lamb fillets and press them in firmly with the palm of your hand, or bat them lightly with a meat mallet or rolling pin.

3. Melt the butter in a large frying pan and when foaming, add the lamb fillets. Cook over a moderately high heat to seal and brown on all sides. Remove them to a plate and set aside.

4. Add the flour to the pan and cook over a moderate heat to brown slightly. Gradually stir in the stock, blending in well and add the sherry and seasoning. Bring to the boil.

5. Drain the fruit, add to the pan and return the lamb fillets. Cover and cook over a gentle heat for about 15-20 minutes, until the lamb and fruit are tender.

6. When the lamb is cooked, remove it from the pan and slice into diagonal pieces about 5mm/¼-inch thick. Arrange on a serving plate and add the cooked fruit.

7. Add the cream to the sauce and bring to the boil. Allow to boil for 1 minute to thicken, then spoon the sauce over the fruit and meat to serve. Garnish with coriander leaves.

TIME: Preparation takes about 25 minutes, with 2 hours soaking time for the fruit. Cooking takes about 30-40 minutes.

VARIATION: Substitute pork fillets or fillet steaks for the lamb neck fillet. Lamb chopes may also be used. Any combination of dried fruit may be used in this recipe.

PREPARATION: When coating the fillets with peppercorns, press firmly so that they stick well in the surface and do not fall off during cooking.

ROAST QUAIL

Quail are delicate, very elegant birds that are perfect as a dinner party dish. They are also easy to prepare and quick to cook – a bonus when entertaining.

SERVES 2

4 dressed quail

4 thin slices pork fat or 4 rashers streaky
    bacon

Fresh sage leaves

60g/2oz butter

4 slices white bread, trimmed to fit under
    the quail

Whole cranberry sauce, or blueberry
    preserve mixed with 1 tsp juice of lemon

1. Remove any pin feathers from the birds and wash them under cold running water. Dry thoroughly inside and out. Lightly salt inside and place a fresh sage leaf inside each quail.

2. Tie the pork fat or bacon rashers around each bird and place in a small roasting tin.

3. Melt the butter over a low heat and brush some over each bird before placing them in a preheated oven at 200°C/400°F/ Gas Mark 6, for about 20-25 minutes. Baste the quail from time to time with the pan juices.

4. Put the remaining butter into a large frying pan and place over a fairly high heat. When hot, add the trimmed slices of bread and brown them on both sides in the butter. Remove to kitchen paper to drain.

5. When the quail are cooked, remove the threads and take off the bacon or pork fat, if wished. Place each quail on a piece of fried bread and serve with the whole cranberry sauce or the blueberry preserve mixed with the lemon juice. Spoon some of the pan juices over each quail before serving.

TIME: Preparation takes about 20-25 minutes and cooking takes about 20 minutes.

VARIATION: Frozen quail may be used in place of fresh quail. Allow to defrost completely before roasting. If neither are available, use 2 pigeons or small poussins and increase the cooking time to 35-40 minutes.

SERVING IDEAS: Serve with new potatoes and fresh peas.

PIGEONS IN WINE

Pigeons make a delicious and inexpensive casserole.

SERVES 2

2 pigeons
¼ tsp each salt, pepper and paprika
1 tbsp oil
15g/½oz butter or margarine
175g/6oz button onions
1 stick celery, sliced
2 carrots, peeled and sliced
2 tbsps flour
200ml/7 fl oz chicken stock
75ml/5 tbsps dry red wine
1 tsp tomato purée (optional)
60g/2oz button mushrooms, quartered or
    left whole if small
60g/2oz fresh or frozen broad beans
1 tbsp chopped mixed herbs

1. Wipe the pigeons with a damp cloth and season them inside with the salt, pepper and paprika.

2. Heat the oil in a heavy-based flameproof casserole and add the butter or margarine. Once it is foaming, place in the pigeons and brown them on all sides, turning them frequently. Remove from the casserole and set them aside.

3. To peel the button onions quickly, slightly trim the root ends and drop the onions into rapidly boiling water. Allow it to come back to the boil for about 1 minute. Transfer to cold water and leave to cool completely. The skins should come off easily. Trim roots completely.

4. Add the onions, celery and carrots to the casserole and cook for about 5 minutes to brown slightly. Add the flour and cook until golden brown, stirring constantly.

5. Pour in the stock and the wine, stirring well. Bring to the boil over a high heat until thickened.

6. Stir in the tomato purée, if using, and return the pigeons to the casserole along with any juice that has accumulated.

7. Partially cover the casserole and simmer gently for about 40-45 minutes, or until the pigeons are tender.

8. Add the mushrooms and broad beans halfway through the cooking time. To serve, skim any excess fat from the surface of the sauce and sprinkle over the chopped herbs.

TIME: Preparation takes about 30 minutes and cooking takes about 50 minutes-1 hour.

VARIATION: The casserole may be prepared with poussins, quail or pheasant. The quail will take only half the cooking time.

SERVING IDEAS: Accompany with broccoli and boulangère potatoes.

SOLE KEBABS

These kebabs make a tasty alternative to the more usual way of cooking fish.

SERVES 2

---

4 fillets of sole, skinned
60ml/4 tbsps olive oil
1 clove garlic, crushed
Juice and finely grated rind ½ lemon
Salt and freshly ground black pepper
2 drops of Tabasco, or pepper sauce
2 small courgettes
½ medium green pepper
Freshly chopped parsley, for garnish

---

1. Cut each sole fillet in half lengthways, and roll each slice up 'Swiss roll' fashion.

2. Mix together the oil, garlic, lemon juice and rind, seasonings, and Tabasco in a small bowl.

3. Put the rolls of fish into a shallow dish and pour over the lemon and oil marinade. Cover the dish and allow to stand in a cool place for at least 2 hours.

4. Cut the courgettes into 0.5cm/¼-inch slices and chop the pepper flesh into 2.5cm/1-inch squares.

5. Carefully thread the marinated sole fillets onto kebab skewers, alternating with the pieces of the prepared vegetables. Brush each kebab with a little of the oil and lemon marinade.

6. Arrange the kebabs on a grill pan and cook under a moderately hot grill for about 8 minutes, turning frequently to prevent them from burning, and brushing with the extra marinade to keep them moist.

7. Arrange the kebabs on a serving dish, and sprinkle with chopped parsley for garnish.

TIME: Preparation takes about 30 minutes, plus marinating time. Cooking takes about 8 minutes.

PREPARATION: After 2 hours marinating, the sole will look opaque and have a partially cooked appearance.

VEAL WITH PEACHES AND PINE NUTS

This dish is quite expensive, but very easy and quick to prepare and cook.

SERVES 2

2 ripe freestone peaches
3 tbsps brandy or sherry
2 tbsps oil
4 small or two large veal escalopes
75ml/5 tbsps dry white wine
Pinch cinnamon
1 small bay leaf
Salt and pepper
15g/½oz butter or margarine
2 tbsps pine nuts
2 tsps cornflour mixed with 1 tbsp water
Pinch sugar, optional

1. Peel the peaches by dropping them into boiling water for about 30 seconds. Remove immediately to a bowl of cold water and leave to cool completely. Use a small, sharp knife to remove the skins.

2. Cut the peaches in half and twist the halves to separate. Remove the stones and place the peaches in a deep bowl with the brandy or sherry. Stir the peach halves to coat them completely.

3. Heat the oil and sauté the escalopes on both sides until golden brown. Pour on the wine and add the cinnamon, bay leaf and salt and pepper then cover the pan. Cook over a low heat for about 10-12 minutes or until the veal is tender and cooked through.

4. While the veal is cooking, melt the butter in a small frying pan and add the pine nuts. Cook over a moderate heat, stirring continuously until they are golden brown. Remove from the butter and set them aside to drain on kitchen paper.

5. When the veal is cooked, remove it to a serving dish and keep it warm. Add the cornflour and water mixture to the pan and bring to the boil, stirring. Cook until thickened and cleared.

6. Remove the peaches from the brandy and slice them. Add the peaches and the brandy to the thickened sauce mixture and bring to the boil. Allow to cook rapidly for about 1 minute.

7. Add the sugar, if using. Spoon the peaches and sauce over the veal escalopes and sprinkle on the browned pine nuts. Serve immediately.

TIME: Preparation takes about 25-30 minutes, cooking takes about 20 minutes in total.

VARIATION: The recipe may be prepared with pork fillet, chicken breasts or duck breasts. Use nectarines or apricots instead of peaches and do not peel them.

PREPARATION: If the escalopes are not very thin, bat them out between 2 sheets of dampened greaseproof paper using a rolling pin.

DUCK IN CAPER SAUCE

A sweet-sour sauce with the tang of capers is a perfect accompaniment to a rich meat such as duck.

SERVES 2

1×2kg/4½lb whole duck, giblets removed
1 clove garlic, crushed
Salt and pepper
1 tbsp oil
45g/1½oz butter
280ml/½ pint chicken stock
140ml/¼ pint water
60g/4 tbsps sugar
1 tbsp vinegar or lemon juice
4 tsps cornflour mixed with 2 tbsps water
90ml/6 tbsps capers

1. Rub the cavity of the duck with the crushed garlic and sprinkle in salt and pepper. Leave to stand for 1-2 hours but do not refrigerate.

2. Heat the oil in a heavy frying pan or roasting pan and when hot add the butter. Prick the duck skin all over with a sharp fork and brown the duck on all sides. Transfer the duck to a saucepan or flameproof casserole.

3. Pour over the stock, cover and simmer over a medium heat for about 1 hour 40 minutes, or until the duck is tender.

4. Meanwhile, heat the water and sugar together slowly in a small, heavy-based saucepan until the sugar dissolves.

5. Once the sugar is dissolved, turn up the heat and allow the syrup to boil rapidly until it caramelizes. Remove from the heat and pour in the vinegar or lemon juice. It will splutter.

6. Add several spoonfuls of the cooking liquid from the duck and set the caramel over medium heat. Allow the mixture to come to the boil, stirring constantly.

7. When the duck is tender, remove it to a heated serving dish. Skim off the fat from the cooking liquid and discard. Mix the cornflour and water together and add several spoonfuls of the duck cooking liquid.

8. Return to the rest of the liquid and bring to the boil. Add the capers and stir over a high heat until the sauce clears and thickens. Add the caramel and stir until the sauce is thick.

9. Cut the duck into portions or serve whole and spoon over some of the sauce. Serve the rest of the sauce separately.

TIME: Preparation takes about 20 minutes with 1-2 hours standing time for the duck. Cooking takes about 1¾ hours.

COOK'S TIP: Pricking the duck skin with a sharp fork allows the fat to run out as the duck cooks. Use this method when roasting or pot roasting to produce duck that is not fatty.

BRAISED RABBIT WITH PEPPERS

Rabbit is available fresh from butchers during the season. Otherwise look for it in freezer cabinets in major supermarkets.

SERVES 2

460g/1lb rabbit joints
1 lemon slice
Flour for dredging
1 tsp dry mustard
1 tsp paprika
1 tsp garlic granules
¼ tsp dried dill
Pinch salt and pepper
Oil for frying
1 small onion, thinly sliced
½ small green pepper, thinly sliced
½ small red pepper, thinly sliced
1 × 400g/14oz can tomatoes
140ml/¼ pint chicken stock
1 bay leaf
1 tbsp dry white wine or sherry (optional)

1. Soak the rabbit overnight with the lemon slice in enough cold water to cover.

2. Drain the rabbit and pat dry with kitchen paper.

3. Combine flour, spices, herbs, and seasoning and dredge the rabbit with the mixture.

4. Heat a little oil in a large frying pan and fry the rabbit on all sides until golden brown. Remove to a plate.

5. Cook the onion and peppers for about 1 minute. Add the tomatoes, stock and bay leaf and bring to the boil.

6. Return the rabbit to the pan and spoon over the sauce. Partially cover and cook over a gentle heat for about 45-50 minutes, or until tender.

7. Add the wine or sherry during the last 10 minutes of cooking, if using. Remove the bay leaf before serving.

TIME: Preparation takes about 25 minutes, plus overnight soaking for the rabbit. Cooking takes about 50 minutes-1 hour.

VARIATION: If yellow peppers are available, use the three colours for an attractive dish.

COOK'S TIP: Soaking the rabbit with lemon overnight helps to whiten the meat and to remove any strong taste.

POUSSINS WITH BITTER CHOCOLATE SAUCE

A small amount of unsweetened chocolate lends a rich depth of colour and a delightfully mysterious flavour to a savoury sauce.

SERVES 2

2 tbsps olive oil
2 single, (small) poussins
Salt and pepper
1½ tbsps flour
1 clove garlic, crushed
140ml/¼ pint chicken stock
2 tbsps dry white wine
1 tsp unsweetened cooking chocolate, grated
Lemon slices to garnish

1. Heat the oil in a heavy-based pan or casserole. Season the poussins and place them, breast side down first, in the hot oil. Cook until golden brown on all sides, turning frequently.

2. Transfer the poussins to a plate and add flour to the casserole. Cook to a pale straw colour.

3. Add the garlic and cook to soften. Pour on the stock gradually, mixing well. Add the wine and bring to the boil.

4. Reduce to simmering, replace the poussins and cover the casserole. Cook for 20-30 minutes, or until the poussins are tender.

5. Transfer the poussins to a serving dish and skim any fat from the sauce. Add the grated chocolate and cook, stirring quickly, over a low heat for 2-3 minutes.

6. Pour some of the sauce over the poussins and garnish with some lemon slices. Serve the rest of the sauce separately.

TIME: Preparation takes about 20 minutes, cooking takes about 25-35 minutes.

BUYING GUIDE: Unsweetened cooking chocolate is not the same as plain chocolate, which must not be used as a substitute. Unsweetened chocolate is available in large supermarkets and speciality shops.

SERVING IDEAS: Serve with rice and a vegetable such as peas or asparagus, or with a green salad.

71

SHERRIED PORK WITH FIGS

Another popular Spanish fruit and meat combination. Figs look especially attractive as a garnish and really complement the sherry sauce.

SERVES 2

460g/1lb pork fillet
25g/¾oz butter or margarine
75ml/5 tbsps medium-dry sherry
140ml/¼ pint brown stock
1 bay leaf
1 sprig fresh thyme
Juice and zest of 1 small orange
2 tsps cornflour
Pinch cinnamon
Salt and pepper
2 fresh figs

---

1. Slice the pork fillet into diagonal pieces about 1.25cm/½-inch thick. Melt the butter or margarine in a large frying pan, and, when foaming, add the slices of pork fillet. Cook quickly on both sides to brown.

2. Pour away most of the fat and add the sherry. Bring to the boil and cook for about 1 minute. Pour on the stock and add the bay leaf and thyme. Bring to the boil and then lower the heat, cover and simmer for about 15-20 minutes, or until the pork is tender.

3. Remove the pork from the pan then boil the liquid to reduce slightly, and add the orange zest. Mix the orange juice and cornflour together. Spoon in a bit of the hot liquid and then return the mixture to the pan.

4. Bring to the boil, whisking constantly until thickened and cleared. Stir in a pinch of cinnamon, salt and pepper. Return the pork to the pan and cook to heat through.

5. If the figs are small, quarter them. If they are large, slice lengthways. Remove the pork to a serving dish and spoon over the sauce. Garnish with the sliced or quartered figs.

TIME: Preparation takes about 25 minutes and cooking takes about 30 minutes.

PREPARATION: Pork fillet can toughen if cooked too rapidly, or over heat that is too high. Simmer gently in the liquid.

SERVING IDEAS: Serve with rice – either saffron or plain.

COUNTRY PORK CHOPS

The sauce in this dish would work equally well with beef, lamb or even chicken.

SERVES 2

1 tbsp oil

2 pork chops

15g/½oz butter or margarine

6 button onions

1 small carrot, peeled and diced

2 tsps flour

280ml/½ pint beef stock

1½ tbsps lemon juice

Salt and pepper

60g/2oz French beans, topped, tailed and
    sliced

60g/2oz fresh peas

1. Heat the oil in a large frying pan. Trim the chops to remove most of the fat. Sauté the pork gently on both sides to brown.

2. Melt the butter or margarine in a medium saucepan. Peel the onions and add to the butter with the carrot. Cook slowly to soften.

3. Sprinkle on the flour and cook to a good golden brown. Add the stock, lemon juice, salt and pepper and bring to the boil. Cook until thickened.

4. Pour the fat from the pork, add the sauce to the pan and cook for about 40 minutes, or until the pork is tender, adding the beans and peas half way through cooking time.

TIME: Preparation takes about 25 minutes, and cooking takes about 50 minutes.

PREPARATION: Brown the flour slowly, stirring constantly for an even colour and to prevent it from burning.

VARIATION: Other vegetables such as diced turnip or potatoes, broad beans, sliced runner beans or mange tout peas may be used instead of the beans and peas.

ROLLED VEAL ESCALOPES

Both Roulades and veal dishes are popular – combine the two and you can't go wrong!

SERVES 2

2 large veal escalopes
4-8 slices German salami or cervalat
15g/½oz butter or margarine
1 tbsp oil
1 tsp chopped sage
3 tbsps white wine
90ml/6 tbsps quark or fromage frais
Salt and white pepper
Fresh sage leaves, for garnish

1. Bat out the escalopes between two sheets of damp greaseproof paper using a meat mallet or rolling pin. When flattened, cut each in half to make squarish pieces.

2. Top each piece with a slice of salami and roll up like a Swiss roll. Secure with cocktail sticks. Alternatively, tie in three places with fine string.

3. Heat the butter and oil in a small frying pan and sauté the meat rolls until evenly browned all over. Sprinkle with the chopped sage and add the wine. Simmer uncovered for about 15 minutes.

4. Remove the rolls, discard the cocktail sticks or string and transfer the rolls to a warm serving dish. Cover and keep warm.

5. Whisk the quark into the pan juices over a low heat until smooth and heated through. Pour this over the rolls to serve, and garnish with fresh sage leaves.

TIME: Preparation takes about 25 minutes, cooking takes about 20 minutes.

VARIATION: Turkey breasts may be used instead of the veal.

WATCHPOINT: Quark will curdle if allowed to boil, so heat very gently.

SERVING IDEAS: Serve with puréed spinach and sauté potatoes. Spinach pasta is also a good accompaniment.

LAMB STEAKS MEDITERRANEAN STYLE

Aubergine is a very popular vegetable in Mediterranean cooking. Its taste is perfect with lamb marinated with garlic and rosemary.

SERVES 2

2 large round bone lamb leg steaks
2 tbsps olive oil
1 clove garlic, crushed
1 sprig fresh rosemary
Black pepper
2 tsps red wine vinegar
1 small aubergine
Salt
2 tbsps olive oil
½ small green pepper, cut into 2.5cm/1-inch pieces
½ small red pepper, cut into 2.5cm/1-inch pieces
1 shallot, chopped
1 tsp chopped parsley
1 tsp chopped fresh marjoram
3 tbsps dry white wine
Salt and pepper

1. Place the lamb in a shallow dish with the oil, garlic, rosemary, pepper and vinegar. Marinate for 1 hour, turning frequently.

2. Cut the aubergine in half and score lightly. Sprinkle with salt and leave to stand for 30 minutes. Rinse well and pat dry.

3. Cut the aubergine into 2.5cm/1-inch pieces. Heat the second measure of oil in a frying pan and add the aubergine. Cook, stirring frequently, over a moderate heat until lightly browned.

4. Add the peppers, shallot, herbs and wine. Bring to the boil and cook rapidly for 5 minutes to reduce the liquid and concentrate the flavour. Set the mixture aside.

5. Meanwhile, place the lamb on a grill pan, reserving the marinade. Cook under a preheated grill for about 10 minutes per side, according to taste. Baste frequently with the marinade.

6. Serve the lamb with the aubergine accompaniment and garnish with fresh rosemary sprigs.

TIME: Preparation takes about 1 hour and cooking takes about 20 minutes.

PREPARATION: The lamb may be marinated overnight.

COOK'S TIP: Sprinkling an aubergine with salt will draw out bitter juices and so give the dish better flavour.

RATATOUILLE

This delicious vegetable casserole from the south of France has become a great favourite the world over.

SERVES 2

---

1 medium aubergine
Salt
2 small courgettes
2 tbsps olive oil
1 Spanish onion
1 medium green or red pepper
1 × 793g/1lb 12 oz can of peeled plum
    tomatoes
1 clove garlic, crushed
Salt and freshly ground black pepper
90ml/6 tbsps dry white wine
2 tsps chopped fresh basil

---

1. Cut the aubergine in half lengthways and score each cut surface diagonally, using the point of a sharp knife.

2. Sprinkle the aubergine liberally with salt and allow to stand for 30 minutes to disgorge. Rinse thoroughly and pat dry on kitchen paper.

3. Roughly chop the aubergine and slice the courgettes thickly. Set them to one side.

4. Halve the onion and cut into thin slices with a sharp knife.

5. Cut the pepper in half lengthways and remove and discard the seeds and white pith. Chop the flesh roughly.

6. Heat the oil in a large saucepan, and sauté the onion for 5 minutes until soft and just beginning to brown.

7. Stir in the pepper and courgettes, and cook gently for 5 minutes until they begin to soften. Remove all the vegetables from the pan and set them aside.

8. Put the chopped aubergine into the saucepan with the vegetable juices. Cook gently until it begins to brown, then add all the other ingredients to the pan.

9. Add the can of tomatoes, the garlic and seasoning to the saucepan along with the sautéed vegetables, mixing well to blend in evenly. Bring to the boil, then reduce the heat and simmer for 15 minutes, or until the liquid in the pan has been reduced and is thick.

10. Add the wine and basil to the pan and continue cooking for a further 15 minutes, before serving straight away, or chilling and serving cold.

TIME: Preparation takes 20 minutes, plus 30 minutes standing time. Cooking takes about 35 minutes.

PREPARATION: Make sure that the disgorged aubergine is rinsed thoroughly to remove any saltiness, otherwise this will spoil the flavour of the finished dish.

COOK'S TIP: If the liquid in the pan is still thin and excessive after the full cooking time, remove the vegetables and boil the juices rapidly until they have reduced and thickened.

NUTTY POTATO CAKES

This recipe is very tasty, and is also the perfect way to use up left over potatoes.

MAKES 6 CAKES

340g/¾lb potatoes
15g/½oz margarine or butter
A little milk
60g/2oz mixed nuts, finely ground
25g/¾oz sunflower seeds, finely chopped
2 tbsps spring onions, finely chopped
Freshly ground black pepper
Wholemeal flour for coating
Oil for frying

1. Peel the potatoes, cut into pieces and boil until just soft.

2. Drain and mash with the butter and milk to a creamy consistency.

3. Add the nuts, seeds, onions and pepper to taste.

4. If necessary, add a little more milk at this stage to give a soft texture which holds together.

5. Form into 6 cakes and coat with some wholemeal flour.

6. Fry quickly in a little oil for 5-10 minutes or until heated through. Drain on kitchen paper and serve hot.

TIME: Preparation takes 10 minutes, cooking takes 25 minutes.

SERVING IDEAS: Serve with a green salad and sliced tomatoes in an oil and fresh basil dressing.

VARIATION: Dry roast the sunflower seeds until golden brown, before grinding. The cakes could also be coated in egg and wholemeal breadcrumbs instead of flour.

Avocado, Orange and Black Olive Salad

A light and colourful salad combining three of Spain's abundant ingredients.

SERVES 2

1 orange
1 avocado
½ small red onion
10 black olives, pitted
Basil leaves

Dressing
2 tsps white wine or sherry vinegar
2 tbsps olive oil
¼ tsp mustard
Pinch of salt and pepper

1. Cut a slice from the top and bottom of the orange and, using a serrated knife, remove all the peel and pith in thin strips. Cut in between the membranes to remove the segments of the orange.

2. Cut the avocado in half and remove the stone. Peel, and cut into slices. Thinly slice the onion.

3. Cut the olives in half and slice them thinly or chop them. Use kitchen scissors to shred the basil leaves finely.

4. Arrange the orange segments, avocado slices, sliced onion and olives on serving plates and sprinkle over the shredded basil leaves. Mix the dressing ingredients together well and pour over the salad to serve.

TIME: Preparation takes about 30 minutes.

COOK'S TIP: Do not peel the avocado more than 30 minutes before serving time unless you prepare the dressing beforehand and coat the avocado with it to prevent discolouration.

VARIATION: Spring onions may be used instead of the red onions. Use different varieties of herbs. Substitute grapefruit for the orange.

SPAGHETTI RICE

An unusual combination of pasta and rice make a deliciously different side dish.

SERVES 2

60g/2oz uncooked long grain rice

60g/2oz uncooked spaghetti, broken into 5cm/2-inch pieces

1½ tbsps oil

2 tbsps sesame seeds

1 tbsp chopped chives

Salt and pepper

200ml/7 fl oz chicken, beef or vegetable stock

2 tsps soy sauce

1 tbsp chopped parsley

1. Rinse the rice and pasta to remove the starch, and leave to drain dry.

2. Heat the oil in a large frying pan and add the dried rice and pasta. Cook over moderate heat until brown, stirring continuously.

3. Add the sesame seeds and cook until golden brown.

4. Add the chives, salt and pepper, and pour over 140ml/¼ pint of the stock. Stir in the soy sauce and bring to the boil.

5. Cover and cook about 20 minutes, or until the rice and pasta are tender and the stock is absorbed. Add more of the reserved stock as necessary. Do not let the rice and pasta dry out during cooking.

6. Fluff up the grains of rice with a fork and sprinkle with the parsley before serving.

TIME: Preparation takes about 25 minutes and cooking takes about 20 minutes or more.

PREPARATION: If wished, once the stock is added the mixture may be cooked in a pre-heated 190°C/375°F/Gas Mark 5 oven. Cook for about 20 minutes, checking the level of liquid occasionally and adding more stock if necessary.

SERVING IDEAS: Serve as a side dish with meat or poultry. Give it an Italian flavour by omitting sesame seeds, chives and soy sauce. Substitute Parmesan and basil instead.

COURGETTE AND PEPPER SALAD

This dish makes an excellent side salad or starter.

SERVES 2

340g/¾lb baby courgettes
½ red pepper, thinly sliced
Juice and zest of ½ small lemon
3 tbsps olive oil
Fresh basil
Salt and pepper
Pinch sugar
Whole basil leaves, for garnish

1. Top and tail the courgettes. Use a cannelle knife to remove strips of peel from the courgettes.

2. Place the courgettes and red pepper in boiling, salted water and cook for 2 minutes. Set aside to drain.

3. Strip the zest from the lemon with a zester. Alternatively, use a swivel peeler to take off strips and then cut the peel in very fine shreds. Blanch for 2 minutes in boiling water.

4. Mix together the oil, lemon juice, chopped basil, salt and pepper and sugar. Pour over the vegetables while they are still warm and sprinkle with the lemon zest. Garnish with whole basil leaves.

TIME: Preparation takes about 25 minutes, cooking takes about 2 minutes.

COOK'S TIP: If serving the salad cold, rinse the blanched vegetables under cold running water and leave to drain thoroughly.

TOMATO AND ORANGE SALAD WITH MOZZARELLA AND BASIL

Tomatoes and mozzarella cheese are a common salad combination. The addition of oranges makes this just a little bit different.

SERVES 2

2 large tomatoes
2 small oranges
120g/4oz mozzarella cheese
4 fresh basil leaves
2 tbsps olive oil
1½ tsps white wine vinegar
Salt and pepper

1. Remove the cores from the tomatoes and slice into rounds about 5mm/¼-inch thick.

2. Cut a slice from the top and bottom of each orange and, using a serrated knife, remove the peel and pith in thin strips. Make sure to cut off all the white pith.

3. Slice oranges into 5mm/¼-inch thick rounds. Slice the mozzarella cheese into the same thickness.

4. Arrange the tomatoes, oranges and mozzarella in overlapping circles, alternating each ingredient.

5. Use scissors to shred the basil leaves finely, and sprinkle over the salad.

6. Mix the remaining ingredients together well and spoon over the salad. Chill briefly before serving.

TIME: Preparation takes about 20-25 minutes.

PREPARATION: Shred the basil leaves just before serving, since they tend to turn black if cut and left to stand.

BUYING GUIDE: Fresh basil and growing basil plants are available in produce sections of most large supermarkets.

MOULDED RICE PUDDING

Serve these individual puddings with a custard sauce, flavoured with orange flower water and decorated with a little fruit purée.

SERVES 2

90g/3oz long-grain rice
2 tsps raisins
2 tbsps sugar
420ml/¾ pint milk
1 egg yolk
60ml/4 tbsps cream

1. Rinse and drain the rice.

2. In a saucepan, add the raisins and sugar to the milk, then stir in the rice. Cook over a low heat, stirring often, until the rice has absorbed all the milk and the mixture has thickened.

3. Add the egg yolk and beat continuously over a low heat for 2 more minutes.

4. Remove from the heat, add the cream and mix in well. Divide the mixture between 2 ramekins and leave to chill in the refrigerator for 2 hours.

5. Turn the puddings out just before serving.

TIME: Preparation takes 20 minutes, plus at least 2 hours chilling time.

VARIATION: The more conventional short-grained rice may also be used for this recipe. Flavour the rice mixture with a little cinnamon or nutmeg.

BLACKBERRY FLUFF

Fresh blackberries combine with yogurt to make a delicious and simple dessert.

SERVES 2

225g/8oz fresh blackberries
140ml/¼ pint natural set yogurt
1 egg white
Sugar to taste
Pieces of angelica and whole blackberries
    to decorate

1. Wash the blackberries thoroughly and place them in a saucepan with no extra water, other than that which is left on their surfaces after washing. Sprinkle over sugar to taste. Cover the pan with a tight fitting lid, and cook over a low heat for 5-10 minutes, stirring occasionally until the fruit has softened. Cool slightly.

2. Press the cooked blackberries through a nylon sieve, using the back of a spoon to press out the juice and pulp. Discard the pips and reserve the purée.

3. Put the yogurt into a large bowl and stir in the blackberry purée until it is smooth.

4. Whisk the egg white until it forms very stiff peaks.

5. Fold this into the blackberry purée, trying not to over mix the ingredients, so as to create an attractive marbled effect.

6. Pile into serving dishes and decorate with the whole blackberries and angelica pieces. Chill before serving.

TIME: Preparation takes about 20 minutes. Cooking takes about 10 minutes, plus chilling time.

PREPARATION: This recipe can also be partially frozen to create a cooling summer dessert.

VARIATION: Use raspberries or strawberries in place of blackberries in this recipe.

MINTED GRAPES

A refreshing dessert to serve after a large meal.

SERVES 2

150g/5oz seedless green grapes
A little Creme de Menthe
60ml/4 tbsps soured cream
Soft brown sugar

1. Halve the grapes and divide equally between two serving glasses.

2. Sprinkle with a little Creme de Menthe.

3. Top with the soured cream.

4. Sprinkle a little brown sugar over and serve at once or chill to allow the sugar to melt into the soured cream.

TIME: Preparation takes 10 minutes.

SERVING IDEAS: Serve garnished with mint leaves.

VARIATION: Use sherry in place of the Creme de Menthe and yogurt instead of soured cream.

SUNBURST FIGS

Fresh figs can make a most attractive dessert in next to no time.

SERVES 2

2 fresh ripe figs
60g/2oz redcurrants in small bunches
3 oranges
½ tsp orange flower water

1. Trim the stalks away from the top of the figs, but do not peel them.

2. Cut the figs into quarters lengthways, taking care not to sever them completely at the base.

3. Press the fig quarters open gently with your fingers, to make a flower shape. Place each fig carefully on a serving plate.

4. Arrange the small bunches of redcurrants carefully in the centre of each fig.

5. Cut 1 of the oranges in half, and squeeze out the juice. Mix this juice with the orange flower water in a small jug.

6. Carefully cut away all the peel and white pith from the remaining 2 oranges.

7. Using a sharp knife, cut the segments of orange away from the inside of the thin membranes, keeping each piece intact as a crescent shape.

8. Arrange the orange segments in between the petals of the fig flower on the serving plate.

9. Spoon equal amounts of the orange sauce over each fig, and chill thoroughly before serving.

TIME: Preparation takes about 15 minutes, plus chilling time.

VARIATION: Use ruby grapefruit segments and blackcurrants in place of the oranges and redcurrants in this recipe.

SERVING IDEAS: Freeze the currants before placing them on the figs, to give an attractive finish to this dessert.

GINGER-FLAVOURED POACHED PEARS

Pears and ginger make a delicious combination.

SERVES 2

2 ripe dessert pears
Juice of ½ lemon
700ml/1¼ pints water
60g/2oz sugar
2 tsps ground ginger

1. Peel the pears and coat them liberally with the lemon juice.

2. Pour the water into a saucepan, and add the sugar. Add the ginger and stir well.

3. Add the pears, cover the pan and poach the fruit over a moderate heat for 15-20 minutes.

4. Once cooked, remove the pears from the pan and allow them to cool. Uncover the pan, increase the heat, and allow the cooking liquid to reduce until it thickens to a light syrup.

5. Allow the syrup to cool and serve it with the cooled pears.

TIME: Preparation takes about 10 minutes and cooking takes about 1 hour 15 minutes.

COOK'S TIP: Coating the pears with lemon juice prevents them from discolouring during cooking.

VARIATION: Use more ginger for a stronger flavour or use cinnamon or whole cloves instead of ginger.

WATCHPOINT: Poaching time will vary according to the ripeness of the pears. Check them from time to time and do not overcook.

POACHED PEACHES WITH SPICES

Wine and spices add a touch of sophistication to a fruit dessert that is simplicity itself to make.

SERVES 2

420ml/¾ pint red wine
225ml/8 fl oz water
60g/2oz sugar
½ vanilla pod
1 juniper berry
Pinch ground cloves
¼ tsp cinnamon
Pinch ground ginger
1 squeeze lemon juice
2 firm peaches

1. Place the wine and water in a saucepan and stir in the sugar.

2. Add all the spices and a squeeze of lemon juice.

3. Add the peaches, cover the pan and poach the fruit on a gentle simmer for about 20 minutes, turning them from time to time.

4. Remove the peaches, increase the heat and boil rapidly to allow the wine and spice mixture to reduce.

5. When the mixture has become thick and syrupy, strain through a fine sieve.

6. Cut the peaches into slices and arrange on two serving plates. Pour over the wine and spice sauce and chill in the refrigerator for at least 2 hours. Serve well chilled.

TIME: Preparation takes about 10 minutes, cooking takes about 40 minutes and the poached peaches should be chilled for at least 2 hours.

BUYING GUIDE: It is best to use very firm peaches for this recipe. Cooking time will vary according to the type of peach.

CHOCOLATE MOUSSE

A favourite throughout France, every chef has his or her own secret recipe for chocolate mousse. This recipe is easy to follow and will be much appreciated by all who taste it.

SERVES 2

175g/6oz dark chocolate

2 tbsps warm milk

2 egg yolks, beaten

60g/1oz sugar

140ml/¼ pint whipping cream, whipped until quite thick

2 egg whites, stiffly beaten

1. Melt the chocolate in a bowl over a saucepan of hot water. Once the chocolate has melted, stir in the warm milk.

2. Beat the egg yolks with the sugar until pale and thick. Stir in the chocolate mixture, mix well and cool for 1 minute.

3. Gently fold in the whipped cream.

4. Then gently fold in the egg whites. Pour the mousse into individual dishes and set in the refrigerator for at least 2 hours before serving.

TIME: Preparation takes about 10 minutes, cooking time is about 8 minutes and setting time is at least 3 hours.

SERVING IDEAS: Decorate the mousses with a few fresh mint leaves or extra whipped cream and grated chocolate.

VARIATION: Add the grated zest of ½ small orange, 1 tsp orange liqueur, or 30g/1oz raisins soaked in 1 tablespoon rum.

MANGO AND COCONUT WITH LIME SAUCE

The taste of mango with lime is sensational, especially when served with the deliciously creamy sauce in this stylish dessert.

SERVES 2

1 large, ripe mango, peeled and sliced
½ fresh coconut
1 egg yolk
2 tbsps sugar
Juice and grated rind of 1 lime
75ml/5 tbsps double cream, whipped

1. Arrange thin slices of mango on plates.

2. Break the coconut half into smaller sections. Grate the white pulp, taking care to avoid grating the brown skin. Use the coarse side of the grater to make shreds and scatter them over the mango slices.

3. Place the egg yolk and sugar in the top of a double boiler or in a bowl. Whisk until very thick and lemon coloured.

4. Stir in the lime juice and place the mixture over simmering water. Whisk constantly while the mixture gently cooks and becomes thick and creamy.

5. Remove from the heat and place in iced water to cool quickly. Whisk the mixture while it cools.

6. Fold in the whipped cream and spoon onto the fruit. Garnish with the grated lime rind.

TIME: Preparation takes about 40 minutes and cooking takes about 8 minutes.

WATCHPOINT: It is important that the water under the sauce does not boil. If it does, it can cause curdling or cook the mixture too quickly, resulting in a poor texture.

PREPARATION: The sauce can be chilled for up to 30 minutes. After that, it may start to separate.

VARIATION: Serve the sauce with other fruit such as papayas, peaches, pineapple or berries.

ORANGES IN RED WINE

*Sunny oranges look and taste beautiful in a rosy red sauce
made with red wine.*

SERVES 2

2 large oranges
120g/4oz sugar
3 tbsps water
75ml/5 tbsps full-bodied red wine

1. Using a swivel vegetable peeler, remove just the peel from the oranges. Be sure not to take off any white pith. Cut the peel into very thin julienne strips.

2. Cut off the pith from the oranges using a small serrated knife. Take off the pith in thin strips to preserve the shape of the fruit. Peel the oranges over a bowl to catch any juice. Slice the fruit thinly and place in a bowl or on serving plates.

3. Place the sugar and water in a heavy-based saucepan over very low heat. Cook very slowly until the sugar dissolves completely and forms a thin syrup.

4. Add the strips of peel and boil rapidly for 2 minutes. Do not allow the syrup to brown. Remove the peel with a draining spoon and place on a lightly oiled plate to cool.

5. Cool the syrup slightly and then pour in the wine. If the syrup hardens, heat very gently, stirring to dissolve again. Allow the syrup to cool completely.

6. Spoon the syrup over the oranges and arrange the julienne strips on top to serve.

TIME: Preparation takes about 40 minutes. The syrup will take about 1 hour
to cool completely.

COOK'S TIP: Add any juice collected while peeling the oranges to the
syrup for extra flavour.

WATCHPOINT: Do not pour warm syrup over the oranges as they
will cook.

PEAR OMELETTE

*The addition of a small amount of ground cloves to this sweet omelette gives it a
very special flavour that marries particularly well with the pears.*

SERVES 2

2-3 canned pears in syrup
6 eggs
1 tbsp double cream
1 tbsp sugar
Small pinch ground cloves
Butter

1. Cut the pears into small, even-sized cubes.

2. Beat the eggs with the cream and sugar. Add the pinch of cloves and stir in the pears.

3. Heat about 30g/1oz butter in an omelette pan. When hot, pour in the egg mixture.

4. Stir the mixture a little in the pan, then cook for a few minutes until set.

5. Shake the omelette loose and brown the top under a hot grill. Serve immediately.

TIME: Preparation takes about 20 minutes and cooking takes 6-10 minutes.

VARIATION: Using a small pan, the egg mixture could be divided to make two individual omelettes.

SERVING IDEAS: Serve with lightly whipped cream.

Index